514
1701

Science at Work in
SOCCER

By Richard Hantula

**Science and Curriculum
Consultant:**
Debra Voege, M.A.,
Science Curriculum
Resource Teacher

Marshall Cavendish
Benchmark
New York

Website: www.marshallcavendish.us

This publication represents the opinions and views of the author based on the author's personal experience, knowledge, and research. The information in this book serves as a general guide only. The author and publisher have used their best efforts in preparing this book and disclaim liability rising directly and indirectly from the use and application of this book.

Other Marshall Cavendish Offices:
Marshall Cavendish International (Asia) Private Limited, 1 New Industrial Road, Singapore 536196 • Marshall Cavendish International (Thailand) Co Ltd. 253 Asoke, 12th Flr, Sukhumvit 21 Road, Klongtoey Nua, Wattana, Bangkok 10110, Thailand • Marshall Cavendish (Malaysia) Sdn Bhd, Times Subang, Lot 46, Subang Hi-Tech Industrial Park, Batu Tiga, 40000 Shah Alam, Selangor Darul Ehsan, Malaysia

Marshall Cavendish is a trademark of Times Publishing Limited

All websites were available and accurate when this book was sent to press.

Library of Congress Cataloging-in-Publication Data
      Hantula, Richard.
            Science at work in soccer / Richard Hantula.
                  p. cm.
            Includes index.
            Summary: "Explains how the laws of science, especially physics, are at work in the game of soccer"—Provided by publisher.
            ISBN 978-1-60870-591-7 (print) — ISBN 978-1-60870-735-5 (ebook)
            1. Soccer—Juvenile literature. 2. Physics—Juvenile literature. I. Title.
      GV943.25.H36 2012
      796.334—dc22   2010052510

Developed for Marshall Cavendish Benchmark by RJF Publishing LLC (www.RJFpublishing.com)
Design: Westgraphix LLC/Tammy West
Photo Research: Edward A. Thomas

Cover: Thierry Henry controls the ball during a 2010 game.

The photographs in this book are used by permission and through the courtesy of:
Front Cover: Andy Marlin/Getty Images.
Getty Images: Simon Bruty/Sports Illustrated, 4; Victor Decolongon, 9; FREDERIC J. BROWN/AFP, 16; RANCK FIFE/AFP, 18; Jim Prisching, 20; Jamie Sabau, 21; Shaun Botterill, 24; Kevork Djansezian, 26. Landov: FRED GREAVES/Reuters, 10; JONATHAN BRADY/EPA, 13. Newscom: imago sportfotodienst, 6.

Printed in Malaysia (T)
135642

CONTENTS

Words defined in the glossary are in
bold type the first time they appear
in the text.

CHAPTER ONE

Goal!

Landon Donovan is about to kick the ball during the 2010 U.S.-Algeria World Cup match.

Landon Donovan made one of the most important and exciting goals in the history of soccer in the United States. The U.S. national team was playing Algeria in the first round of the 2010 World Cup. Neither team had scored, and there were only about three minutes left in the game. The Americans faced a desperate situation. A tie would knock them out of the tournament.

Then, in just 12 seconds, the United States took the ball down the length of the field and scored. The U.S. attack began right after an Algerian player tried to head the ball into the U.S. goal. The U.S. goalkeeper made the stop and then threw the ball to Donovan near midfield. Donovan, moving the ball with his feet, pushed it up the right side of the field. He passed it forward to a teammate, who right away sent it across the field toward the front of

What's in a Name?

Soccer is the most popular sport in the world. But most people around the globe don't call it soccer. They call it football. People in the United States, however, use *football* as the name of a different game. So Americans say "soccer" when they mean the game with lots of kicking. In soccer, unlike American football, usually only the goalies touch the ball with their hands or arms.

The name *soccer* first appeared in England in the 1800s. An organization was formed there to develop rules for the sport. It was called the Football Association, and some people began calling the sport "association football." Using the *soc* in association, the name became soccer for short.

Today, the organization that governs both men's and women's soccer around the world still uses the word *association* in its name. It is usually called FIFA. This stands for its French name, *Fédération Internationale de Football Association*, which means "International Federation of Association Football."

the goal, in hopes that another American could take a shot. The Algerian goalie rushed out. He dove to the ground and cut off the pass. But the ball got away from him and rolled toward Donovan, who kicked the ball into the Algerian net. The U.S. team won and moved on to the next round.

Feet, Hands, and Head

Many of soccer's basic features showed up in those few seconds of action. The aim of the game is to score by putting the ball into the opponent's goal. Players usually kick the ball with their feet or hit it with their heads, although other parts of the body, such as the chest, can touch it. With two exceptions, players are not allowed to handle the ball with their hands or arms.

Goalies can use their arms and hands as long as they don't go outside the area around the goal called the penalty area. Other players can use their hands only when a ball goes out of bounds and needs to be thrown back in.

A professional soccer match normally has 90 minutes of playing time. During that time, players—and the ball—are always on the move. But the ball can move in a lot of different ways. How fast it goes and where it goes depend on how it is kicked or hit.

England's John Terry hits the ball with his chest during 2010 World Cup play.

Professional-Level Soccer Field

50–100 yards (45–90 meters)

Touch Line

Penalty Area

Goal

Goal Line

100–130 yards (90–120 meters)

Under FIFA rules, the length and width of a soccer field can vary.

There is a branch of science that can explain why soccer balls move the way they do. This branch of science is called **physics**. It studies such things as the motion of objects.

Newton's Laws

Some of the most important ideas in physics were developed by the English scientist Isaac Newton in the 1600s. Newton described three basic rules, or laws, that explain the motion of everyday objects such as soccer balls. His laws show how an object's motion is related to the things that cause it to move. These things push or pull the object. They are called **forces**.

PHYSICS FACT

First Law of Motion

If an object is at rest, it will stay at rest unless a force acts on it. If an object is moving, it will keep on moving in the same direction and at the same speed unless a force acts on it.

The first of Newton's laws says that if an object is moving, it will keep on moving at the same speed and in the same direction unless some force acts on it. The law also deals with objects that are not moving at all. These objects have zero speed. They are often said to be "at rest." Newton's first law says that they will stay at rest unless some force acts on them. For example, a soccer ball that is just lying on the ground is at rest. For it to move, a force—such as a player's kick—has to act on it.

If a soccer ball is flying through the air, it will keep on going forever until a force makes its motion change. There are lots of forces that might do this. One of them is Earth's **gravity**, which is constantly pulling downward. Also, the air acts against the movement of the ball through it. This **resistance** by the air is called **drag**. Drag slows the ball down. Players can change a ball's speed or direction, too. When they kick it or hit it, they apply a force to the ball.

Physicists often say Newton's first law using the idea of **velocity**. Many people use the word *velocity* to mean simply "speed," but for physicists it means the combination of speed and direction of motion. So Newton's first law of motion says simply that a moving object will keep on moving at the same velocity unless some force acts on it.

A different way to look at the first law of motion uses the idea of **inertia**. Inertia is an object's resistance to a change in motion. Because of inertia, a moving ball will keep on moving at the same velocity, unless some force acts

to overcome this resistance. Also, a ball at rest will stay at rest, unless a force overcomes its inertia.

Energy at Work

Another key physics idea that helps explain what goes on in a soccer match is **energy**. Energy is the ability to do work. It comes in different forms. One form is the energy of a moving object. This is called **kinetic energy**. Heat is also a form of energy. One of the most basic ideas of physics is called **conservation** of energy. This means that energy cannot be created or destroyed. It can, however, be changed from one form to another.

When a soccer player kicks the ball, the player's kicking leg has kinetic energy. When the kicker's foot hits the ball, it pushes into the ball, changing the ball's shape. The space inside the ball gets smaller. The air it contains gets squeezed. But this air pushes back, making the ball round again.

When the kicker's foot changes the shape of the ball, some of the kicker's kinetic energy turns into heat. A lot of the kinetic energy goes to press together, or compress, the air in the ball. This air stores the energy for a very short while—until the ball springs back to its normal shape.

Energy in a stored form is called **potential energy**. When the ball springs back to its round shape, the potential energy turns into kinetic energy, and the ball flies off the kicker's foot.

CHAPTER TWO
Putting Forces to Work

Mia Hamm (9), one of the greatest players ever in U.S. women's soccer, dribbles around a defender in a 2004 game.

S uppose a player needs to send the ball a long way or wants to make a really fast-moving shot on goal. This requires hitting the ball with a lot of force. A powerful kick with the top of the foot can do the job. At other times power may be less important than accuracy—kicking the ball in the right direction. In these situations, players tend to use the side of the foot—usually the instep, or curved inner side. This produces a softer kick but gives the kicker more control over where the ball goes.

Dribbling, in which the player's feet just tap the ball, gives even more control. The player's feet use much less force than in kicks. But dribbling can be very useful. It lets a player keep control of the ball while moving the ball down the field or simply while faking out a member of the other team.

But what if the ball is in the air and the player can't reach the ball with a foot? Or what if the ball is in the air and there's no time to kick it before a member of the other team gets to it? In situations like these, players often hit the ball with their head. Experts say children should avoid heading the ball. A kid's skull—the bony part of the head—is not as strong as an adult's. It, and the brain inside it, can be more easily damaged. For skilled adult players, however, a header can be very useful. If properly done, it can be a safe way of hitting the ball with some force. It can even be used to aim the ball in a particular direction.

Newton's Second Law

All these moves and plays use different amounts of force. They may apply the force in different directions. It might seem that they don't have very much in common. But in fact, they do.

PHYSICS FACT
Second Law of Motion
When a force acts on an object, the greater the force, the greater the acceleration it gives to the object. If the same force is used on objects of different masses, objects with less mass receive more acceleration.

Newton came up with a law that helps explain what happens. It is called the second law of motion.

The second law describes the change that a force makes in an object's velocity (its speed and direction). Physicists have a special name for this change. They call it **acceleration**. Some people use the word *acceleration* to mean just an increase in speed. But that's not the way the word is used in physics. In physics, acceleration can be an increase or a decrease in an object's speed, or it can be just a change in the object's direction of motion. All these changes are examples of what physicists call acceleration.

Newton's second law tells how much acceleration a force can give an object. The amount of acceleration depends on two things. One of them is the strength of the force. A stronger force will give an object more acceleration than a weaker force will. The acceleration also depends on the **mass**, or amount of matter, in the object. Suppose the same force is applied to two objects with different masses. Newton's second law says that the object that has more mass will receive less acceleration.

Mixing Forces
So an object's mass determines how a force affects it. But that's not the full story of what happens when a force acts on an object. Usually there is more than one force at work. Some forces may be small and unimportant. Others can be very important indeed. To see what the result of a force

The greater the force a player uses when kicking the ball, the greater the acceleration the ball will get.

might be, it is necessary to look at the effects of all the major forces at work.

Forces that completely oppose each other—that is, that act in opposite directions—tend to cancel each other out. If one force is stronger than the other, the weaker one reduces the effect of the stronger one. When they are of equal strength, they completely cancel each other out. Think of what happens when two teams play tug-of-war. The teams are pulling in opposite directions. If they pull with equal force, the rope they are pulling on doesn't move at all. If one team is stronger—pulls on the rope with a greater force— the rope will move toward that team. But the stronger team has to work hard—the rope will not move as easily as when the other team is not pulling in the opposite direction.

Mass Really Matters

People sometimes confuse an object's mass with its weight. An object's mass and weight are related, but they are different things. Mass is the amount of matter in the object. It represents the object's inertia. Weight is actually a measure of gravity's pull on the object. Gravity pulls more strongly on objects with more mass than on objects with less mass. So it is true to say that heavy objects— objects with a high weight—have more mass than do light ones, which have a low weight.

But gravity is different on different worlds. The Moon's gravity, for example, is much weaker than Earth's. An object that weighs 66 pounds (30 kilograms) on Earth will weigh only about 11 pounds (5 kilograms) on the Moon. The object's mass on the Moon, however, is the same as its mass on Earth.

When forces act in the same direction, their effects add together. For example, when a ball is kicked into the air, gravity keeps pulling downward on it. Meanwhile, the air also opposes the ball's upward motion. In other words, drag pushes down on the ball. The two forces—gravity and drag—act together to keep the ball from going as high as it would if there were no gravity and air.

Something more complicated happens when forces act in different, but not completely opposite directions. The stronger forces contribute more to the final result, and the weaker ones contribute less. To see how this works, suppose a ship is on the ocean and is heading east. Its engines are supplying the power needed to push it forward. The ship keeps going straight eastward until it comes to a current—a stream of moving water—that is going in some direction other than east. The current will apply a force to the ship. As a result of this force, the ship's motion will no longer be directly eastward. The new direction of the ship will depend on the current's strength and direction.

Back at You

Newton's third law of motion describes one more aspect of what happens when a force acts. The third law says that if an object applies a force to another object, the second object applies an equal force to the first. The third law is sometimes said in a slightly different way: for every action there is an equal and opposite reaction.

To see how the third law works, think about a force in action. Take, for example, Earth's gravity. Because of its pull, a soccer ball flying through the air sooner or later falls down to the ground. The third law says that the ball pulls on Earth with the same amount of force that Earth pulls on the ball. It's easy to see the result of Earth's pull: the ball gets accelerated downward. What about the ball's pull on Earth? There really is nothing to see. Newton's second law explains why. Remember, it says that when a force acts on an object, the greater the mass of the object, the smaller the acceleration it receives from that force. The mass of Earth is enormous. Earth is so huge that the acceleration it receives from the ball's pull is practically zero.

PHYSICS FACT

Third Law of Motion

When one object applies a force to a second object, the second also applies an equal force to the first. In other words, for every action there is an equal and opposite reaction.

Better Headers

Heading provides a good example of the importance of a couple of key physics ideas. One is Newton's third law. The other is **momentum**. Momentum is a measure of an object's motion. It depends on both the object's mass and its velocity.

Melissa Tancredi of Canada uses a diving header to score a goal at the 2008 Olympic Games.

Headers are done when the ball is in the air. The ball may or may not be moving fast. If it is going fast, it will have a lot of momentum, even though its mass is small. If the speeding ball hits a player, it will deliver a fair amount of force. In parts of the body like the head, this can cause injury if the player is not careful.

But even if the ball is moving slowly and has little momentum, there is a risk of injury when a player heads it incorrectly. The player doing the header wants to transfer momentum from his or her body to the ball. This requires hitting the ball with the head. But the ball has to obey Newton's third law. It will apply to the player's head the same force that the head applies to the ball.

Most coaches say that the safest way to head the ball is to hit it with the forehead. The bone in this part of the head is thicker than the bone in other parts of the skull. So the forehead is better able to absorb the shock of impact.

Another reason for using the forehead is that it is flatter than other parts of the head. This means that a larger area will come into contact with the ball, resulting in a little better control of the play.

Players can head the ball with more force by doing things to increase their momentum. One thing they can do is to involve their whole body—all their mass—in the play. If they just stand on the ground, only part of their mass takes part in heading the ball. So players often jump or sometimes even dive toward the ball. This increases the amount of their mass that affects the ball. It also boosts their velocity, producing an additional increase in momentum.

Head Injuries

Headers may not be unusually dangerous for skilled older players who know how to do them correctly. They can be a problem for young players whose skulls are not yet fully developed. Actually there are a number of situations in soccer that can cause head injuries to players of all ages, including the serious brain injury called a concussion. These situations include colliding with another player, falling down and hitting one's head on the ground, hitting one's head on a goalpost, and being accidentally hit in the head by a flying ball. Anytime one of these things happens and symptoms of possible head injury appear—such as pain or unusual behavior—the player should be checked by a doctor and follow the doctor's advice very carefully. A player should never ignore symptoms or hide them (perhaps to avoid missing playing time). Head injuries that are not properly treated can cause very serious problems.

CHAPTER THREE

Kicking, Sticking, Spinning

Spain's Andrés Iniesta kicks the winning goal in the 2010 World Cup championship game.

The championship game of the 2010 World Cup pitted Spain against the Netherlands. Both teams played tough defense. After a full 90 minutes, they were still tied at 0-0. They continued to play. In the 108th minute, a member of the Netherlands team was sent off the field because of a penalty. A few minutes later, Spain's Andrés Iniesta managed to get open to the right of the Netherlands goal. A teammate passed the ball to him. Iniesta shot from about 8 yards (7.3 meters) out. The goalie stretched to reach the ball and just missed it as it sped into the net. Spain won, 1-0.

The shot was relatively simple. Iniesta just blasted the ball into the goal. Still, the shot relied on the same basic idea as more complicated kicks: the passing of kinetic energy and momentum from the player to the ball.

Making a Kick

To make a kick, a player turns potential energy into kinetic energy. The potential energy is the energy stored in the food eaten by the player. The player's muscles use this energy to move the kicking leg. This gives the leg kinetic energy and momentum. The kick passes a lot of this energy and momentum over to the ball. The ball typically ends up moving faster than the leg. This is because kinetic energy depends on

Running for Momentum

When players want to make a long throw, a short running start can be a big help. It adds to the momentum received by the ball. Goalkeepers often use it to make throws. Players throwing the ball in from the edge of the field also sometimes use a running start for more momentum. Running starts are also often used in making free kicks and corner kicks. These plays begin with the ball at rest. The kicker runs up to the ball in order to increase the momentum he or she can give it.

The Bicycle

Different situations call for different kinds of moves. There even are situations where a bicycle can come in handy. A bicycle kick, that is. It is difficult to do. But it was a favorite of Pelé, the Brazilian often called the greatest soccer player of all time.

The bicycle kick can be done only when the ball is already in the air. The kick can be a useful move when the player happens to be facing in the direction opposite to where he or she wants the ball to go. In other words, the move begins with the player's back facing the target of the kick.

The player jumps up while turning his or her body backward— sort of like a somersault. One leg goes up in the air. Then the other leg goes up to kick the ball. The player's legs look almost like they are pedaling a bicycle.

Jozy Altidore, playing for the United States in a match against Poland, attempts a bicycle kick.

both mass and speed. The ball is much smaller in mass than the kicker's leg. So if it picks up most of the leg's kinetic energy, it has to move much faster than the leg.

Of course, in a game the situation can be a bit more complicated. The ball may be already in motion when it is kicked. If so, it already has some momentum. This momentum works together with the momentum from the kicker to help determine where the ball goes.

To make a really long or powerful kick, a soccer player needs to swing his or her whole kicking leg from the hip. The whole leg has a lot of mass and can produce a lot of force when moving fast. When a player swings his or her whole leg, the top of the foot is used for the kick.

Kicking with the front of one's big toe is usually a bad idea. This kind of kick provides very little control over where the ball goes and may even injure the toe.

Sticking to Things

One of the most important forces at work in soccer acts when an object moves across a surface. The surface resists the object's motion. This resistance is the force called **friction**. Friction tends to slow down the moving object. Strong friction may even bring the object to a stop. A ball rolling on a soccer field goes slower and slower because of friction. When goalkeepers catch a ball, friction between their hands and the ball helps them grab it.

Friction's strength depends on the materials in the object and the surface. Professional goalies wear special high-friction gloves that help them get a good grip on the ball. A ball rolling on dry grass will meet more friction than a ball rolling on a field that is wet or snowy. Water and snow are more slippery than dry grass: they offer less friction.

Goalies often use special high-friction gloves to help them hold on to the ball.

Playing the Angles

The goalkeeper's job is to keep the other team from putting the ball into the goal. But the front of the goal is a huge area. In international play it is 24 feet (7.32 meters) wide, and the bottom of the crossbar is 8 feet (2.44 meters) above the ground. If the goalie stands at the goal line, it is impossible for him or her to guard this entire area—unless some teammates help.

But what if no teammates are on hand? What should the goalie do if a player from the other team starts a one-on-one attack? The best thing is to move partway out toward the ball. This is called reducing the angle. It lets the goalie block a larger portion of the goal. It reduces the part of the goal that the attacker can shoot at.

Still, the goalie may not manage to stop the ball. One problem is **reaction time**. In the World Cup final, Iniesta's shot took less than a second to get to the net. But the goalie had even less time to try to reach the ball. When he saw the kick, his brain and his body took time to react to it. The best goalies have a fast reaction time, but it is always greater than zero.

The goalie also has to be careful. Coming too far out might open the way for the attacker to score with a chip shot. This is a shot that rises over the goalie's head and then comes back down in the net.

Spinning Ball

When a soccer ball is kicked or thrown in some direction, it moves in that direction. But at the same time, the ball may also have another type of motion. It may spin. When a ball spins, it turns around an imaginary line that goes through the center of the ball. This line is called the ball's **axis**.

Soccer balls don't always spin, but they often do. Suppose a ball is kicked into the air right at its exact center. It will fly off with no spin. A kick at any other point on the ball will tend to give it a spin. Throwing the ball can also give it a spin.

Spin is important because it can change what a ball does. Suppose a ball has **topspin**. In topspin, which can occur when the ball is kicked above its center, the front of the ball

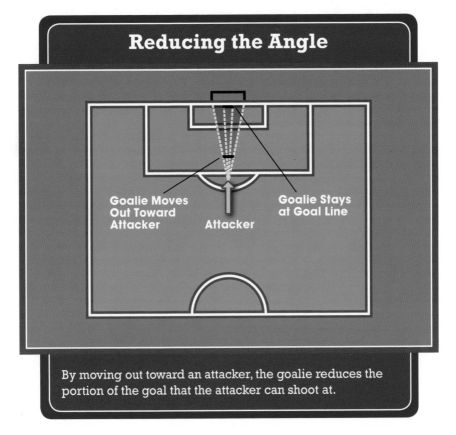

Reducing the Angle

Goalie Moves
Out Toward
Attacker

Attacker

Goalie Stays
at Goal Line

By moving out toward an attacker, the goalie reduces the portion of the goal that the attacker can shoot at.

keeps rolling down and toward the back. This can be useful in a free kick where a player wants to kick over defenders and get the ball into the goal. The topspin interacts with the air to make the ball dip. If the kicker is in luck, the ball will go over the defenders and then dip as it approaches the goal—so that it goes under the crossbar.

Backspin is the opposite of topspin and can occur when the ball is kicked below its center. Backspin can be useful in passing the ball with a bounce. When the ball bounces on the ground, friction from the ground affects the ball's motion. If the ball has backspin, friction makes it move more slowly after it bounces. This can make it a little easier for the player receiving the pass to handle the ball.

CHAPTER FOUR

Air Bending

Roberto Carlos of Brazil gets ready to kick the ball during the 1997 match between France and Brazil.

Roberto Carlos of Brazil made one of the most famous goals ever. Some people call it the super goal. To those watching it, it seemed to happen by magic. It came on a free kick in a match between the Brazilian and French national teams in 1997.

Carlos placed the ball on the ground about 38 yards (35 meters) in front of the French goal. The French team's goalkeeper, Fabien Barthez, stood right in front of the net. Also, a few French players made a "wall" at a spot between the ball and the goal line. They stood together in a row so their bodies partly blocked the right side of the goal.

Carlos then ran up to the ball and kicked it. He aimed it toward the right side of the goal. It went around the right of the wall and seemed likely to go too far right and miss the net. A ball boy standing on that side ducked. But the ball suddenly curved toward the left. Barthez, surprised, simply stood by as the ball went into the net. He also had thought that the ball would go to the right of the goalpost. Instead, it magically produced a score.

Of course it wasn't really magic that did the job. It was physics. Various forces acted on Carlos's ball. Combined, they bent its path toward the left. Roberto Carlos is not the only player who can kick the ball so that it curves. Many others can do this, including British star David Beckham. Carlos's 1997 shot, however, was especially spectacular. He kicked it from an unusually great distance, and it made an unusually sharp curve.

Shot Like a Cannonball

It's easy to name some of the chief forces that affected Carlos's ball. One was the powerful force with which he kicked the ball. This gave it a lot of momentum.

DAVID BECKHAM

Many players are good at making soccer balls curve around a wall of defenders. But David Beckham (shown here in a 2009 game) may be the most famous. His skill was the basis for the 2002 movie *Bend It Like Beckham.*

Beckham was born in 1975 in London, England. As a boy, he dreamed of becoming a soccer player. He practiced hard and showed enough talent to sign his first professional contract when he turned 14. Beckham played for several years for the English club Manchester United. By 2002 he was the highest-paid player in the world. He moved on to Spain's Real Madrid in 2003 and to the Los Angeles Galaxy in 2007. He served as captain of the English national team from 2000 to 2006.

After the ball was put into motion, the force of gravity kept trying to pull it down. The ball acted like a cannonball or any other object shot into the air. Such objects are called **projectiles**. When launched, they move both upward and forward. Their velocity can be divided into two parts. One part is in the upward, or vertical, direction. The other is in the forward, or horizontal, direction.

Gravity affects only the vertical part of a projectile's velocity. Because of gravity's constant pull, the projectile's upward speed keeps slowing until it reaches zero. The projectile then starts falling downward. Gravity's pull tries to make it fall faster and faster.

During the time it rises and falls, the projectile also keeps going forward. The distance it travels after its highest point is roughly the same as the distance it travels before its highest point. Its path is similar to a special curve called a parabola.

The path is only roughly like a parabola because another important force also acts on the projectile: air resistance keeps slowing it down. So the distance it travels after the high point is actually shorter than the distance traveled before the high point.

These projectile forces—gravity and air resistance— affect all soccer balls that are kicked or thrown into the air. But some balls also curve toward the side as they fly.

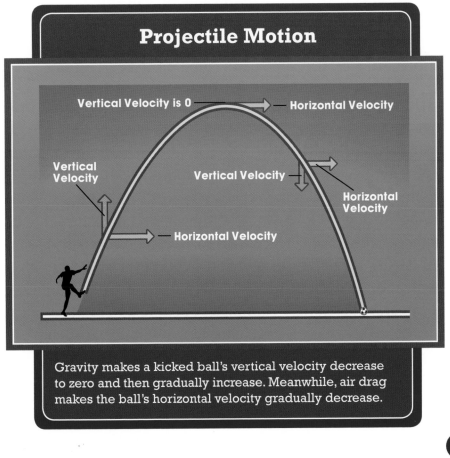

Projectile Motion

Vertical Velocity is 0 — Horizontal Velocity

Vertical Velocity

Vertical Velocity

Horizontal Velocity

Horizontal Velocity

Gravity makes a kicked ball's vertical velocity decrease to zero and then gradually increase. Meanwhile, air drag makes the ball's horizontal velocity gradually decrease.

Players such as Carlos and Beckham are experts at making this happen. Their kicks must be affected by other forces.

Magic from the Air

Among the additional forces at work, one of the most important is produced by a combination of the motion of the air and the ball. Air flows around the ball as it flies. This results in certain forces on the ball. If the ball happens to be spinning, these forces can work together with the spin to create a new force. It is called a **Magnus force**. The Magnus force tries to push the ball in a new direction. This direction is at a right angle, or perpendicular, both to the ball's direction of flight and to the axis of the ball's spin.

The Magnus force is not always strong enough to cause a noticeable effect. The ball visibly curves only if it is moving at a certain speed and spinning at a certain rate.

The Magnus Force in Action

The airflow past the ball works together with the spin in rather complicated ways. To get an idea of how the Magnus force happens, start by picturing an airplane. It can stay up in the air because of the way its wings affect the air they move through. Air has weight. It pushes on objects in it with a force called air pressure. This force can be very strong. At Earth's surface, air usually pushes on every object in it with a force of about 14.7 pounds per square inch (about 1 kilogram per square centimeter). People don't notice this force because they are used to it, but it is there. An airplane's wing is shaped in such a way that air flowing above it flows faster than air flowing below it. As a result, the air pressure above the wing is less than the pressure below. Since the upward force from below is greater than the downward force from above, the plane gets lifted up. Something similar leads to the Magnus force on a spinning ball. The ball's spin affects the airflow so that the air pressure right next to one side of the ball is stronger than the pressure on the other side. When Carlos and Beckham want to make the ball curve, they kick it off-center so that it has a sideways spin. This causes the ball to curve in the direction of the spin. For example, to make the ball bend to the left, the player kicks the ball a bit to the right of its center. This gives the ball a counterclockwise spin (as seen from above the ball). This spin results in a Magnus force that makes the ball curve toward the left.

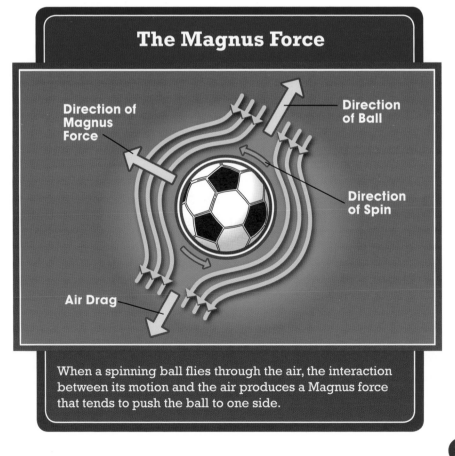

The Magnus Force

Direction of Magnus Force

Direction of Ball

Direction of Spin

Air Drag

When a spinning ball flies through the air, the interaction between its motion and the air produces a Magnus force that tends to push the ball to one side.

GLOSSARY

acceleration: A change in velocity. As a measurement, it is the rate at which velocity changes.

axis: In a spinning ball, the imaginary line running through the ball's center around which the ball turns.

backspin: A type of spin in which the back of a ball rolls down and toward the front. It is the opposite of topspin.

conservation: In physics, the idea that something cannot be destroyed. For example, energy is always conserved, but it may change from one form to another.

drag: Air resistance; a force that slows an object moving through the air.

energy: In physics, the ability to do work.

force: Anything that causes a change in the velocity of an object, such as a push or a pull.

friction: A force resisting the movement of an object across a surface.

gravity: A force that pulls objects toward the center of Earth.

inertia: The tendency of an object to resist being accelerated. A force has to be applied in order to put into motion an object that is at rest or to change the velocity of an object that is moving.

kinetic energy: The energy of a moving object.

Magnus force: A force that acts on a moving object that is rapidly spinning. It pushes the object sideways relative to the axis of the spin.

mass: The amount of matter in an object.

momentum: A measure of an object's motion. It equals the object's mass multiplied by its velocity.

physics: The branch of science dealing with matter and energy. Scientists who work in physics are called physicists. They study such things as moving objects.

potential energy: Stored energy.

projectile: An object that has been put into motion in the air by some force.

reaction time: The time it takes for a person to respond to something.

resistance: Opposition to the movement of an object.

topspin: A type of spin in which the front of a ball rolls down and toward the back. It is the opposite of backspin.

velocity: In physics, the speed and direction of a moving object. Some people use the word to mean simply "speed."

FIND OUT MORE

BOOKS

Bazemore, Suzanne. *Soccer: How It Works*. Mankato, MN: Capstone Press, 2010.

Crisfield, Deborah W. *The Everything Kids' Soccer Book: Rules, Techniques, and More about Your Favorite Sport!* Avon, MA: Adams Media, 2009.

Gifford, Clive. *Soccer*. New York: Marshall Cavendish Benchmark, 2010.

Goodstein, Madeline. *Goal! Science Projects with Soccer*. Berkeley Heights, NJ: Enslow, 2009.

Hornby, Hugh. *Soccer*. New York: DK Publishing, 2010.

Hyde, Natalie. *Soccer Science*. St. Catharines, Ontario: Crabtree, 2009.

WEBSITES

www.fifa.com
This is the official website of FIFA, the international organization that oversees soccer around the world and conducts the World Cup and other tournaments. It includes information on the rules and history of soccer (or, as most of the world calls it, football).

www.howstuffworks.com/soccer.htm
Part of the HowStuffWorks website, this webpage gives basic facts about soccer, including its history and how it is played.

www.mlsnet.com
This is the official website of Major League Soccer, the top-level professional soccer league in the United States and Canada.

http://news.bbc.co.uk/sport2/hi/football/skills/default.stm
The British Broadcasting Corporation put together this website, which includes tips and videos on nearly all aspects of soccer (called football on this website).

www.soccerballworld.com
This website provides information about the history of soccer balls, what they are made of, how to care for them, and much more.

INDEX

About the Author

Richard Hantula has written, edited, and translated books and articles on science and technology for more than three decades. He was the senior U.S. editor for the *Macmillan Encyclopedia of Science*.